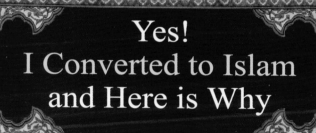

Yes!
I Converted to Islam
and Here is Why

Adapted by

Darussalam Research Division

DARUSSALAM
GLOBAL LEADER IN ISLAMIC BOOKS
Riyadh • Jeddah • Sharjah • Lahore
London • Houston • New York

First Edition: August 2001

Supervised by:
ABDUL MALIK MUJAHID

Headquarters:

P.O. Box: 22743, Riyadh 11416, KSA
Tel: 00966-1-4033962/4043432
Fax:00966-1- 4021659
E-mail: darussalam@naseej.com.sa
Website: http:// www.dar-us-salam.com
Bookshop: Tel & Fax: 00966-1-4614483

Branches & Agents:

K.S. A.
● Jeddah: Tel & Fax: 00966-2-6807752
● Al-Khobar: Tel & Fax: 00966-3-8692900

U.A.E.
● Tel: 00971-6-5511293 Fax: 5511294

PAKISTAN
● 50 Lower Mall, Lahore
  Tel: 0092-42-724 0024 Fax: 7354072

● Rahman Market, Ghazni Street
  Urdu Bazar, Lahore
  Tel: 0092-42-7120054 Fax: 7320703

U. S. A.
● Houston: P.O. Box: 79194 Tx 77279
  Tel: 001-713-722 0419 Fax: 001-713-722 0431
  E-mail: Sales @ dar-us-salam.com
  Website: http:// www.dar-us-salam.com

● New York: 572 Atlantic Ave, Brooklyn
  New York-11217
  Tel: 001-718-625 5925

U.K.
● London: Darussalam International Publications Ltd.
  226 High Street, Walthamstow, London E17 7JH U.K.
  Tel: 0044-208 520 2666 Mobile: 0044-794 730 6706
  Fax: 0044-208 521 7645
● Darussalam International Publications Limited
  Regent Park Mosque, 146 Park Road, London Nw8 7RG
  Tel: 0044-207 724 3363

AUSTRALIA
● Lakemba NSW: ICIS: Ground Floor 165-171, Haldon St.
  Tel: (61-2) 9758 4040 Fax: 9758 4030

MALAYSIA
● E&D BOOKS SDN.BHD.-321 B 3rd Floor, Suria Klcc
  Kuala Lumpur City Center 50088
  Tel: 00603-21663433 Fax: 459 72032

SINGAPORE
● Muslim Converts Association of Singapore
  Singapore- 424484
  Tel: 0065-440 6924, 348 8344 Fax: 440 6724

SRI LANKA
● Darul Kitab 6, Nirmal Road, Colombo-4
  Tel: 0094-1-589 038 Fax: 0094-74 722433

KUWAIT
● Islam Presentation Committee
  Enlightment Book Shop
  P.O. Box : 1613, Safat 13017 KUWAIT
  Tel: 00965-244 7526, Fax: 240 0057

BANGLADESH
● 30 Malitola Road, Dhaka-1100
  Tel: 0088-02-9557214, Fax: 0088-02-9559738

Yes! I Converted to Islam and Here is Why

In the Name of Allâh,
the Most Gracious, the Most Merciful.

"Truly, the religion with Allâh
is Islâm…" (3:19)

Contents

Publishers Note

All praise is due to Allâh, and may He exalt the mention of our Prophet 鐵, his household and Companions.

Allâh has chosen Muhammad 鐵 to be His last Messenger to convey His lost Message to mankind. This means that Islam is not restricted to one particular race, rather, it is a universal message to mankind at large. It the only *Deen* of which Allâh approves. He says:

> "And he who seeks a *Deen* other than Islam, it shall not be accepted from him and he shall be among the losers on the Day of Resurrection." (3:85)

Throughout ages Islam has received a great response to the point that there is not a single city in the world which is void of Muslims. This is due to the fact that whoever applies reason while studying Islam, cannot help but accept it out of conviction.

In this book Darussalam has compiled sample testimonies of those who studied Islam objectively and converted to it conscientiously. It is not that Islam needs such testimonies in order to verify its authenticity. Our intention is to let those who have not yet contemplated converting to Islam share the insights of those who already have by reading their testimonies, and to know that Islam is a faith which is suitable for all ages and applicable until the end of time.

Our ultimate objective is to pass on the Message and to help deliver as many people as we can from the torment of Hell, expecting our reward only from Allâh the Exalted to Whom we are grateful.

Abdul Malik Mujahid
General Manager Darussalam

Views of the Converts in brief about Islam

> Moderation and temperance are
> keynote traits in Islam

The simplicity of Islam, the powerful appeal and compelling atmosphere of its mosques, the earnestness of its faithful adherents, the confidence inspiring realization of the millions throughout the world who answer the five daily calls to prayer - these factors attracted me from the first.

The broad-minded tolerance of Islam for other religions recommends it to all lovers of liberty. Muhammad admonished his followers to treat well the believers in the Old and New Testament; and Abraham, Moses, Jesus are acknowledged as co-Prophets of the One God. Surely this is generous and far in advance of the attitude of other religions.

Moderation and temperance in all things, keynote of Islam, won my unqualified approbation.

Col. Donald S. Rockwell
U.S.A.

> Islam alone can satisfy the needs of every member of the human family

Christianity must go the way of all things, and henceforth perish and forever to make room for the True Religion of God to mankind, and that is Islam, which is Truth, sincerity, toleration, looking to the interests of man and pointing him to the Right Way. Islam alone can satisfy the needs of every member of the human family, and Muslims are the only people among whom can be found the "True Book of Brotherhood" in reality and not mere "make-belief" as in Christianity.

Sir Jalaluddin Lauder Brunton

England

> Islam alone offers the solution to present-day problems

To the Western mind, the chief appeal of Islam must be its simplicity. Admittedly, there are one or two other faiths which are as easy of approach but they sadly lack the vitality of the Faith of the Prophet (may Allâh bless him), and the spiritual and moral elevation which it offers.

Islam must also appeal by virtue of its tolerance... Strangely

Christian intolerance awakened my first interest in Islam.

The Churches are utterly incapable of grappling with present-day problems. Islam alone, offers the solution.

John Fisher
Newcastle

Islam has always attracted me both by its simplicity & by the devotion of its followers

Since adopting Islam as my faith I feel that I have come to a turning point in my life, and to account for this, I want to give you some idea as to why I have become a Muslim. I have subjected myself to what I might call a self-psychological analysis.

Islam had always attracted me both by its simplicity and by the devotion of its followers ... I was taught to regard all religions other than Christianity as blasphemous and their adherents as heathens.

Islam has given me a very practical method of breaking down the barrier of materialism in one of the Five Pillars of Faith, namely 'Prayer.' The Muslim prayer keeps me constantly aware of my duty to Allâh, to my soul, and to my fellow creatures.

Khalid D'Larnger Remraf

Views of the Converts in brief about Islam

> The purity and simplicity of the Islamic Faith & its obvious Truth made a special appeal to me!

The purity and simplicity of the Islamic Faith, its freedom from dogma and sacredotalism and its obvious Truth made a special appeal to me. The honesty and sincerity of the Muslims, too, are greater than anything I have seen in Christians.

Another beauty of Islam is its equality. It is only Islam that has real equality maintained between man and man and no other religion has anything like it. The Faith of Islam generates unity.

The *Deen* of Islam is also the cleanest religion in the world because Muslims have to wash the exposed parts of the body five times a day, a practice not found in any other religion of the world.

A.W.L. Van Kuylenburg

(Known as M.A. Rahman)

> I have accepted Islam because it fits in so well with my own ideas

A man becomes a truer Christian or a Jew by way of Islam than by any way advocated by the Christian or Jewish

people today.

In Islam, there is tolerance and an acknowledgement of universal brotherhood. So, I may say, that I have accepted Islam because it fits in so well with my own ideas about Allâh and His beautiful plan. It is the only Faith I really can understand. Indeed, such is its simplicity and beauty that even a little child can understand it.

Amina Le Fleming

> If Britain and Europe were converted to Islam, they would again be powerful forces for good

There is no version of Christianity which is really satisfactory. Christians believe that because of the fall of Adam and Eve, all human beings are born in a state of original sin, and are unable by their own actions to merit Heaven. Muslims, however, do not believe that people are punished for the sin of Adam and Eve. They believe that all human beings are born of innocence, and can only lose their hope of Heaven by their own sins when they are old enough to be guilty of deliberate wrongdoing.

If Britain and Europe were converted to Islam, they would again be powerful forces for good. British and European Muslims are some of the best.

Khadija F.R. Fezoui

England

Views of the Converts in brief about Islam

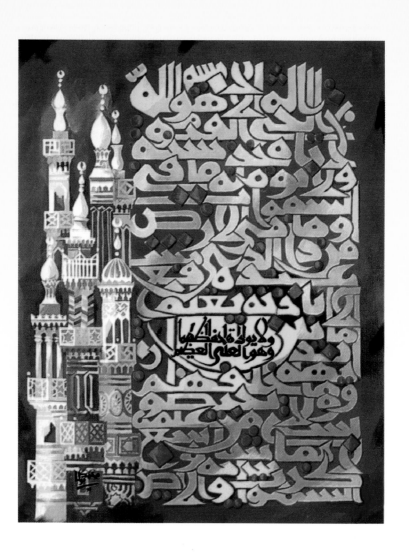

Views of the Converts in brief about the Noble Qur'ân

> The Noble Qur'ân contains what
> every soul requires

Since my youth, I have been greatly impressed by Islamic civilization in all its aspects, its poetry and architecture; and very often I have told myself that a people who could give to the world so vast a treasure of beauty and significance in every branch of culture, must also have attained the highest levels both in philosophy and religion.

In my enthusiasm for Islam, I began to study all religions, from the most ancient to those of the present day, comparing each with the other, and subjecting them to very close

criticism; and little by little, I became convinced that the Muslim worship is the True Religion, and that the Noble Qur'ân contained what every soul requires for its spiritual elevation.

Count Eduardo Gioja

Italy

> I studied a Muslim translation of the Noble Qur'ân and was astounded to read such noble precepts and inspiring passages!

I studied a Muslim translation of the Noble Qur'ân, and was astounded to read such noble precepts and inspiring passages, such wise and practical advice for everyday life. It made me wonder why I had been taught that Muhammad was a false prophet, and how I had not heard the truth about this wonderful religion earlier.

Islam, if sincerely followed, must bring that peace to the mind and body which the world itself needs, and create a perfect social order.

Hasan V. Mathews

Views of the Converts in brief about the Noble Qur'ân

> The Noble Qur'ân is full of truths, and its teachings are so practical and free from dogmatic tenets and mysteries!

As a Roman Catholic, I had the opportunity of studying the Catholic faith to a great extent. I was doing my best to convince myself that Catholicism was the only true faith, but alas! its mysteries, dogmas and the compulsory 'must believes' did not permit me to remain quiet. I started my search for the Truth and remained engaged in this for many years quite silently.

In Hinduism and Buddhism, I found such 'vacant spots' that the only alternative left to me was to study Islam. At one time, I really held Islam in abhorrence. I had no Muslim friends, for Islam was so repulsive to me that I did not want even to associate with its adherents. Little did I dream that ... books on Islam would make a new man of me. I was gradually becoming so observed in the lovely teachings of Islam that it did not take me long to go earnestly further into it. I began to love Islam because of its straight and non-mysterious path. It is clean and simple, yet so full of deep studies that I soon felt the inevitable was drawing nigh.

The Noble Qur'ân, some passages of which I read, simply struck me with wonder, for I had the idea that there was nothing to rival the Bible. I found, however, that I was hopelessly mistaken in this. Indeed, the Noble Qur'ân, is so full of truths, and its teachings so practical and free from dogmatic tenets and mysteries, that I was daily being drifted into the religion of 'Peace and Love' which Islam certainly is.

Mumin Abdur-Razzaque
Selliah, Ceylon

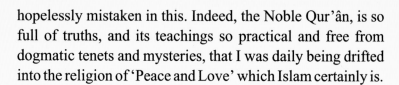

The more I read the Qur'ân, the more I became convinced that it is the only true religion

I studied Christianity, but, even stripped of all the trappings of ritualism and superstitions, it could not satisfy me because I could not accept the fundamental principles of Christianity – the divinity of Jesus, and the doctrine of the original sin and redemption.

So naturally I turned to Islam. I say naturally because I always had a sort of nostalgia for Islam, brought up, as I was in its atmosphere, from my earliest childhood. It was like coming home, and the more I read the Qur'an, and the books on Islam by Muslim writers, the more lucid and convincing,

the more I became convinced that it is the only true religion, a religion for peoples who think ad do not want to shut their eyes to the realities of life and the discoveries of science.

Mrs. C. Sa'eeda Namier

> The superiority of the Qur'ân over the Bible to me lay in its all-embracing universality!

The superiority of the Qur'ân over the Bible to me lay in its all-embracing universality in contrast to the narrow, rigid, nationalism of the Jewish Scriptures which is one of the reasons, why Jew to this day have never been able to outgrow their tribal mentality. As this broad, all-encopassing universality in approach, makes for the superior morality, it has exerted a drastic effect on the historical development of these faiths and the civilizations shaped by them.

Maryam Jameelah Begum
(Formerly Margaret Marcus)

Views of the Converts in brief
about the Noble Qur'ân

The Noble Qur'ân is a mine of infinite wealth

I learnt of this worldwide brotherhood, possessing no racial or class distinctions; of the 'Oneness' of God; of the respect and reverence ascribed to all the former prophets of God; and of the true meaning of Islam - Peace. It sounded wonderful, and I yearned to know more of this faith, which is so practicable and broad-minded.

To me the Holy Qur'ân is a mine of infinite wealth; with such guidance - for every day of one's life - no one need fear or go astray. I am a much happier person than before, though many trials have come to me because of my changed views.

Miss Rahima Griffiths

At the Threshold of Islam

Why I embraced Islam

Why did I embrace Islam? My only convincing answer to this question is that Almighty Allâh in His Glory helped me in admitting the Greatest Truth and testifying to the biggest reality to the world. I, however, know fully well that human nature and its disposition refuse to be convinced of certain facts and realities without satisfactory proofs and cogent arguments. Keeping in view man's nature, I feel that this reply of mine would not satisfy those who are not inclined towards, nor do they feel any interest in, searching for the Truth, nor those on whom the light of truth has not dawned. I am, therefore, left with no alternative but to reduce to writing some of the reasons and causes that induced me to embrace Islam and to stick to it. While staying in a European society, I express my joy and jubiliation, that the people living in these societies do not change their religion nor do they deviate from their faith for the sake of economic, political or social

temptations nor do they rush to embrace any religion, unless it works as a strong incentive and an effective factor to open up their hearts and generate spiritual tranquillity. Otherwise, they remain contented with infidelity and apostasy.

Here then, if one pauses to consider, one will come to the conclusion that my own act, or for that matter, the act of any individual in the European society, of embracing Islam does not imply earning economic profits or attaining social advantages. The matter is rather the other way around. Firstly, we, the peoples of the European society, attach no importance to religious matters. However, if there is anyone from among the European society who cares for religion, the aim of such a one is nothing but to find God. As such, my own interest in Islam meant nothing but search for the Truth and the direction of right thinking.

A desire of search for the Truth arose in my heart. A longing to find the Truth crept into my self. This was when I saw that many doubts and misgivings had been growing and rising in my imagination and memory about the Christian beliefs and its fundamentals. At the same time, the capacity of Christianity fell short of providing resistance and protection against those doubts and misgivings. Christianity used to press that all its tenets be admitted without proof and argument.

To cite an example, my heart is not inclined to accept the Christian belief that Glorious Almighty Allâh sent Prophet Jesus Christ for the whole world as an expiator of the sins of

At the Threshold of Islam

all the slaves of Allâh. It also did not appeal to me that the entire humanity was sullied with various colours of sins including disobedience, and all the sins of the slaves of Allâh were forgiven, following the crucifixion of Jesus Christ. I also felt that Allâh Himself inevitably possesses full power to save His slaves and to keep them away from committing sins and crimes. I also felt that He has all the might to forgive, on His own, the sins of His slaves without any explanation being necessary. Thus, Glorious Allâh does not need any explanation to forgive the sins of His slaves. Even so, I felt that the belief of making the Prophets a ransom for the sins of the entire humanity is tantamount and similar (God forbid) to imputing motives of wrongdoing and injustice to Almighty Allâh. On the other hand, man may commit sins and crimes without any hesitation and hitch. Whenever I expressed these doubts to any Christian scholar or priest, he advised me to banish from my mind these doubts and instigated me to accept those beliefs of Christianity, without any reservation. They strongly pressed me to give up the idea that they are not convincing, so that these doubts and views may not grow nor flourish in my mind. The desire to search for the Truth had been constantly growing till I arrived at a very critical juncture which denies all faith and (revealed) laws.

In those days I had the opportunity to come across a religious and capable Muslim who, inspite of being charmed by the glamour of European culture and civilization, used to take pride in stating that he was a Muslim. He affirmed that, through the blessings of Islam, he enjoyed contentment of the heart and mental tranquillity. On the other hand, a feeling of

weirdness and disgust against the name of religion had got hold of my heart. This assertion of his filled my heart with a sense of astonishment and I was drowned in a sea of thought: Is there a religion which provides the heart's contentment and mental peace to those who profess and follow it? This idea induced me to acquire knowledge about Islam and its disciplines. Now I claim by dint of my studies that Islam is the immortal religion of Allâh which has the ability to elate the hearts of those who submit to it. It helps them in all their affairs and difficulties. It removes all doubts and suspicions arising in the hearts of the people from the teachings and beliefs of other religions.

One of the most important teachings of Islam that influenced my heart is that it does not call man to submit to it without thinking and reflection. On the other hand, man has been invited to think and reflect deeply and clearly and weigh every Islamic belief on the scale of understanding and wisdom before accepting it. In Islam, Allâh the All-Mighty is the source and fountainhead of justice. It is, therefore, not possible that Allâh should make any man a ransom for the sins of all mankind. According to the Islamic belief, Allâh the All-Mighty possesses all eternal, exalted attributes and is free from all shortcomings and defects. For this reason, Islam maintains that this notion is against wisdom and beyond conception, that Allâh the All-Mighty has bestowed on man the liberty to commit sins and has given him free rein to indulge in offences under the theory of expiation.

At the Threshold of Islam

These are, thus, the eternal teachings of Islam which cleared up from my mind the tendency of hate against religion and religious regulations. They led me to the conclusion that religion is a permanent, independent code of law which ensures for man everlasting prosperity, eternal honour and endless victory and triumph.

At this critical stage, on the one hand, I made an extensive, intensive and analytical study of Islam, from the standpoint of an abiding law of life. On the other hand, I focussed my keen attention on the question: how Islam provides man with peace of mind and tranquillity of the self in the present age in which new problems and contemporary issues crop up from day to day. So, when my heart came at rest and my self calmed down from both directions, I embraced Islam. For lack of space it is not possible for me to express all the impressions and the emotions that my mind received. It is, however, necessary to clarify the lessons with which I was inspired in Islam: It is that Islam directs the entire humanity towards the real goal of its creation and guides it to achieve those lofty aims. It conveys the message of peace and security to the human society; establishes bonds of fraternity and equality among them and obliterates all differences and disputes including those of colour, race and nationality. It rescues them from social and economic exploitation and from all other shapes of racial discrimination. It leads them to a vast expanse of right guidance and a path that is uniform and straight.

Not only does Islam oppose stagnation and deterioration in life, but it also calls all mankind to achieve advancement and development. It allows the individual to earn money and wealth and attain industrial and commercial development. It gives him the right to wages and awards as long as these activities are lawful and are not ill-gotten. So Islam is a complete and comprehensive evolution. It embraces all aspects of revolution and excellence. It is a belief that advances, along with the entire humanity, in the right and straight direction, where man feels that he is a member of an international community, understands his duties and is solicitous about the demands of life.

When about ten years ago I embraced Islam, peace and tranquillity returned to my distracted, troubled and defiant nature.

Praise, gratitude and thanks to Allâh that I am enjoying a life full of contentment and satisfaction.

Dr. Abdul Karim Herbert

At the Threshold of Islam

My adherence to Islam!

As a Doctor of Medicine, and a descendant of a French Catholic family, the very choice of my profession has given me a solid scientific culture which had prepared me very little for a mystic life. Not that I did believe in Allâh, but that the dogmas and rites of Christianity in general, and of Catholicism in particular, never permitted me to feel His presence. Thus, my unitary sentiment for God forbade my accepting the dogma of the Trinity, and consequently of the Divinity of Jesus Christ.

Without yet knowing Islam, I was already believing in the first part of the *Kalimah* — *Lâ ilâha illallâh* (There is no true God except Allâh), and in these Verses of the Qur'ân.

So, it was first of all for metaphysical reasons that I adhered to Islam. Other reasons, too, prompted me to do that. For instance, my refusal to accept Catholic priests, who, more or less, claim to possess on behalf of God the power of forgiving the sins of men. Further, I could never admit the Catholic rite of Communion, by means of the host (or holy bread), representing the body of Jesus Christ, a rite which seems to me to belong to totemistic practices of primitive peoples, where the body of the ancestral totem, the taboo of the living

Ones, had to be consumed after his death, in order better to assimilate his personality. Another point which moved me away from Christianity was the absolute silence which it maintains regarding bodily cleanliness, particularly before prayers, which has always seemed to me to be an outrage against Allâh. For if He has given us a soul He has also given us a body, then we have no right to neglect it. The same silence could be observed, and this time mixed with hostility with regard to the physiological life of the human being, whereas on this point Islam seemed to me to be the only religion in accord with human nature.

The essential and definite element of my conversion to Islam was the Qur'ân. I began to study it, before my conversion, with the critical spirit of a Western intellectual, and I owe much to the magnificient work of Mr. Malek Bennabi, entitled Le Phenomene Coranique, which convinced me of its being divinely revealed. There are certain Verses of this Book, the Qur'ân, revealed more than thirteen centuries ago, which teach exactly the same notions as the most modern scientific researches do. This definitely converted me to the second part of the *Kalimah*: '*Muhammad-ur-Rasulullah*' (Muhammad is the Messenger of Allâh).

This was my reason for presenting myself at the Mosque in Paris, where I declared my faith in Islam and was registered there as a Muslim by the *Mufti* of the Paris Mosque, and was given the Islamic name of 'Ali Selman.

I am very happy in my new faith, and proclaim once again:

"I bear witness that there is no true God except Allâh; and I bear witness that Muhammad is Allâh's servant and Messenger."

Ali Selman Benoist
(France)
Doctor of Medicine

What led me to embrace Islam

Professor Arthur Alison is the Head of the Department of Electrical and Electronic Engineering in the University of London. For several years he had been the President of the British Society for Psychological and Spiritual Studies. In the course of his study of religions, he got acquainted with Islam. When he compared Islam with the religions and creeds he had studied, he found it suited his inborn nature and satisfied his requirements.

He was invited to the First Islamic International Conference on the Medical Inimitability held in Cairo from the 29th September to the 6th of October 1985, under the auspices of the Egyptian Medical Syndicate. In the conference, he presented a paper on the psychological and spiritual methods

of therapy in the light of the Holy Qurân, in addition to another paper on sleep and death in the light of Verse 42 of *Sûrah Az-Zumar* (39) which he presented in collaboration with Dr. Mohammed Yahya Sharafi. The facts, presented in the conference, were an eyeopener to him.

At the concluding session of the Conference attended by Shaikhul- Azhar Jad Al-Haq, the Egyptian Minister of Awqaf, Dr. Mohammed Ahmady and Dr. Mohammed Yahya Sharafi and in the presence of Press Reporters and T.V. Correspondents, Professor Arthur Alison stood to declare that Islam is the religion of truth and inborn nature with which Allâh has created man. Then he uttered the two testimonies (*Shahadatain*) saying that he bears witness that there is no God, but Allâh and that Muhammad is the Prophet of Allâh.

In an interview given to the Arabic weekly, '*Al-Muslimoon*' of London, he narrated the story of his conversion to Islam saying:

> "In the course of my study of psychology and related subjects as the President of the British Society for Psychological and Spiritual Studies, I got acquainted with religions. I studied the religions of Hinduism, Buddhism and some other religions and creeds. When I studied Islam, I compared it to other religions.

> "During the Conference on 'Medical Inimitability in the Qur'ân,' I could realize that the difference was great. Then I was convinced that Islam is the most proper religion that befits my inborn nature and conduct. In my heart, I had felt that there is a God controlling the Universe. He is the Creator.

At the Threshold of Islam

"Therefore, when I studied Islam, I found that it did not conflict with reason and science. So, I believed that it was the revealed religion from One and Only Allâh. As I witnessed the truth, I uttered the two testimonies. The moment I uttered it, I was overwhelmed by a strange and ineffable feeling mingled with ease, comfort and satisfaction."

Prof. Arthur Alison

Why I embraced Islam

I was brought up in the religion of the Church of England, and hardly remember any time when Sunday was not English Sunday, a thing that is—or has become—almost an institution in this country. Also, it was a day when one was being constantly told not to do this thing, and not to do the other. One was severely reprimanded for "being naughty on Sunday," as if it was worse to do wrong on a Sunday than any other day. In the morning, church was the first order of the day; and when I began to argue on certain points connected with the Christian doctrine, or to question its accuracy, not only was nobody able to answer any of my questions, but I was told it was wrong to make inquiries. I was told God had written the Bible; but when I asked, had He written it with a pen, where was the original document, and had anyone seen Him do so, such questions raised pious horror in the mind of my governess. It was not only dull, but extremely irksome for me to have to follow a religion which from its very root beliefs was so entirely illogical and impossible. Not only did I wish to love the God I worshipped, but I was extremely interested in Him, and eager to know more about Him as He really was. I could never reconcile the idea of an All-Mighty or All-Merciful God allowing His Son such an ignominious and shameful death as a means to save the world—for the

very fact of the crucifixion proved to me that such a God who, could do such a thing could be neither "All-Mighty" nor "All-Merciful." If He were All-Mighty, there was no need for Him to require the assistance from anyone else, human or divine, and if He were All-Merciful, He could not willingly allow a perfectly innocent person to suffer for the sins committed by other people who were guilty. Not only that, but I had only to look around me at the sins and wrongs going on in the world, to see that it had in no way been saved by the death of an innocent man; and on discussing the matter with people I found that half the people who professed to be Christians did not really believe all they were supposed to, but held to it, because it was so much easier not to change or to bother to think for themselves. The Sunday afternoons were spent in my being obliged to learn the catechism or a hymn by heart. How much better would it have been had I been told some real and ennobling truth about my Creator, than to be made to repeat in a parrot-like fashion the rules of a doctrine I did not believe in. I was relieved that at all events I was not confirmed, for that seemed to me to be the culminating point of the whole thing. I hated the words "body and blood of Christ," even if in the Protestant faith they were only meant allegorically and theoretically, and not as the "real body and blood of Christ" as in the Catholic Church. The idea of the sacraments worried me greatly, but I secretly determined, I would never be confirmed. Sunday evening we finished up with hymns, and to refuse to come and join in, and sing them, was considered most disobedient, only to be accepted with the alternative of going to bed if I

couldn't behave like the rest. Thus, Sunday was a long day that dragged wearily through, and it was such a strain—what with Sunday expressions, Sunday behaviour, Sunday occupations, hymn-singing and church—that it often ended in my behaving worse than on an ordinary weekday. The Bible I always heartily disliked—it gave me neither comfort, consolation, nor the smallest help whatever. When I grew up, I found it such a mass of contradictions, extraordinary fables and impossibilities, that one felt disgusted and saddened instead of being helped and comforted. Those who were supposed to be in a position to interpret it—clergymen, for instance—failed entirely when I questioned them concerning it. What, therefore, could be the use of a book that was so wrapped up in fable and fancy that no one could explain it? The Bible is the result of a collaboration of dozens of different authors. Science and geology prove that the Beginning, as described in Genesis, is an utter impossibility. We have also proof that King David never wrote the Psalms, and that various other parts of the Bible attributed to different people were not written by them. Thus then, since so many people have had the task of inventing the Bible, who is to be believed? The Holy Book of Islam—the Qur'ân—on the contrary, has come to us through only one man, namely, the holy Prophet Muhammad. It has never been altered, twisted, paraphrased and transcribed as the Bible, but has remained true to its original copy. The Qur'ân appealed to me. The doctrine of Islam appealed to me. These, then, are some of the reasons why I have embraced Islam, a religion that is comforting, uplifting, and sustaining, and why I have

At the Threshold of Islam

discarded one that has never, from the first word I learnt of it, ever inspired, encouraged, or uplifted me at all.

Ameena Annie Spieget

An English Lady

Why I am a Muslim

My early religious training was in the Christian faith. This, however, was a matter of birth, not of choice—our early religious training is generally in the faith of our parents. Later in life, our religion is usually accepted as a matter of fact. We, however, question and examine everything except our religious faith, particularly if it is Christianity.

The Christian Bible, being the textbook of Christianity, is a book which I have read many times. I doubt if there is a person who does not shudder while reading its pages, filled as they are with blood-curdling slaughter, rapine and destruction, along with its tales of incest, rape and other vile obscenity. Indeed, after reading the Bible one cannot help but wonder as to the nature of this "God of the Christians."

Almost every Christian home contains the Bible, but it is generally used as a mantelpiece decoration. If it were the custom of the printer to deliver this book with its edges

At the Threshold of Islam

uncut, it would, no doubt, remain so for many years. Charles Francis Potter, D. D., in his book "The Story of Religion" wrote: "The Christian Bible may be 'the book nobody knows' in America, but the Qur'ân is the book everybody reads in Islam." Yes, indeed, and it is an advantage to Christianity that the Bible is "the book nobody knows." The Bible was the first cause in leading me away from Christianity.

Having lost all interest in Christianity, I began a study of other world religions, as well as various "ologies" and "isms." All this was followed by agnosticism and atheism. However, there is, I believe, in mankind an innate certainty deeply rooted which persists in proclaiming the fact that there is an Allâh, a Divine Creator, Master of the universe. But not the God who glories in bloodshed, atrocities and sensuousness. It was this "innate certainty" which caused me to return to a further study of religion.

I found that Islam appeals to one's reason; it does not contain the pessimism of Buddhism; it is not void of Divinity like Shintoism or Confucianism, nor is it a money-made religion. I found that it invites and encourages the pursuit of knowledge. The pages of history are filled with facts citing the hindrances which Christianity placed in the pathway of progress and civilization. It was a traditional saying of the Prophet Muhammad of Blessed Memory that "who so pursue the road of knowledge; Allâh will direct him to the road of *Jannah*; verily the angels spread their arms to receive him who seek after knowledge; verily the

superiority of a learned man over a mere worshipper is like that of the full moon over the stars."

I do not hesitate to state that were Islam better known in the Western World, it would have astound the civilized world by its gain in adherents. The reason why it is not better known, is that it is with difficulty that one can obtain authorized or even unbiased literature pertaining to the Islamic faith. However, I am sure, time will rectify this condition.

In bringing this article to an end, I wish to state that I am very happy to add my voice to the millions who proclaim to the world *Lâ ilâha illallâh, Muhammad-ur-Rasulullah*—There is no true God but Allâh and Muhammad is His Messenger.

Harry E. Heinkel

How I came to Islam

As a child I had won several prizes for proficiency in the Scriptures, but the more I learnt of my religion, the more sceptical I became of it. At fourteen years of age I went through the rites of "Confirmation" in my church. By going through this ceremony I expected to banish all my doubts and

fears, and to be able to face my troubles aided by the Spirit of God (which, I was informed, would enter my body through the fingers of the Bishop who laid his hands on my head). Instead of strengthening my belief, however, this ceremony only added to my growing conviction that my religion was a mass of foolish superstitions and ridiculous rites.

By the time I had left school and gone to a University, this suspicion had become a certainty; the Christian Church, as I had been shown it, meant little or nothing to me.

I could admire Jesus as a noble saint and martyr, to make a God of him seemed to me to be decidedly unreasonable, and certainly not in keeping with his own teachings. Although I found it a simple matter to discover fallacies in the creed I had discarded, it was more difficult for me to discover a more logical one to take its place. Christianity was a mass of contradictions and superstitions. Rationalism offered at best a very unsatisfactory belief: and there appeared to be no reasonable religion to combine the best elements of all the different faiths I had read and heard about!

I almost despaired of finding an established creed which would include all the ideas I had formulated; and for a long time I tried to satisfy myself with vague beliefs of my own.

One day I chanced on a copy of "Islam and Civilisation" by Khawaja Kamal-ud-Din.

As I read it, I realised that nearly all my own beliefs were included in the doctrine the little volume expounded.

At the Threshold of Islam

The broad outlook of Islam, as opposed to the intolerance of the Christian sects, the learning and culture in the Islamic countries of the Middle Ages, compared with the ignorance and superstition of other lands at that time, the logical theory of compensation as against the Christian idea of Atonement, were a few of the points that first struck me. Later I came to realise that here was a faith as wide as humanity itself, ready for the guidance of rich and poor alike, and able to break down all barriers of creed and colour. Through the Muslim Mission, I obtained some more detailed information of the teachings of the Holy Prophet. The *Imam* of the Mosque at Woking was always ready to answer any of my criticisms, and his friendly and interesting letters did much to encourage me to inquire further about this faith that was being revealed to me. I was so confident in Islam and its ability to fulfill all spiritual needs, that after a month or two I almost regarded myself as a Muslim.

I wisely decided, however, not to rush matters, but to consider this new religion of mine from all angles before I finally adopted it for my guide in life.

It has always been a theory of mine that things easily come by are easily lost, and likewise beliefs lightly adopted are often just as lightly discarded. Therefore, I read as many criticisms of Islam as I could, specialising in books written about the Holy Prophet and his message by Western writers. Some of what I read was not always favourable to Islam, but the better and more unprejudiced writers were generally forced to admit the value of Islam and its doctrine to civilization, and in some cases even to testify to the truth of its message.

I put my beliefs to a further test by discussing them with a learned friend of mine whose opinions I have always valued very highly. I discovered to my surprise that he shared most of my views,—in fact he was a Muslim without realizing it himself! There must be thousands of people like him; people who have discovered Islam for themselves not realizing that their own ideas were taught by Muhammad hundreds of years ago. During the past few months my faith in Islam has grown, and I am now supremely confident that I have found the truth at last. Now that I have a religion, I can really understand and follow, I feel that I can face life with renewed vigour. Incidentally, since I found my real faith, I have had more good fortune and happiness in my daily life than I have had at any time previously. It is one of my ambitions to bring the light of Islam to some of those who are as dissatisfied with their own beliefs as I was, and to give them that peace of mind which is the keynote of our great and glorious creed.

T.H. Mc C. Barklie

Conversion to Islam

In my studies about Islam, I found out that Islam teaches the purest form of monotheism in the fullest sense of the word. God has no sharer and partner. He is the Creator, Cherisher,

At the Threshold of Islam

Sustainer and Sovereign of the entire universe. All our sincere worship and reverence belong to Him alone and that all the beautiful names of God are His exclusive perfect attributes which nobody of His creation has the right to arrogate them to himself. To associate partners or take other gods besides Him contradicts the Oneness of God.

Indeed, Islam has shown me the Truth, the right kind of Belief and the correct path that leads man to his Creator. So, after nine months of exposure to Islam, I was fully convinced of the truth without any reservation, I embraced Islam on June 3, 1985. In fact, I had no difficulty in embracing Islam. As you know, man, being a rational creature, must not only uphold the truth but is duty bound to declare and defend truth under all circumstances. It would be an act of obstinacy, whimsy, shame and irreligious to ignore the truth which is tantamount to betrayal of the Creator to Whom we owe our very existence. Had God willed to wipe us out, He could have done it anytime, but He has specific Divine purpose for each of us. God has manifested what He requires from us when He said:

> "And I (Allâh) created not the jinn and humans except to worship Me (Alone)." (*Sûrah Az-Zâriyât*, 51:56)

Praise is to Allâh Who has been kind to bring me to the correct and straight path. All this has happened because of the Noble Book—Qur'ân— which answered all my doubts and strengthened my faith in Islam.

I met a European, Mr. Mathews, who had embraced Islam

years before. He told me a lot about the Faith of Islam, and the simplicity and truthfulness of it made a very deep impression on me. Just before I came home, I had the very great pleasure of reading the Noble Qur'ân, which influenced me profoundly, and it was then that I decided to embrace Islam. I had already asked Mr. Mathews about the procedure to be followed, and so on my arrival in England, I wrote to Lord Headley, who was kind enough to give me the information I required.

On the whole, I think the main cause of my embracing Islam was the fact that I found it to be the only religion where faith and truth are truly predominant.

I may add that I do not like the pomp of other religions, because it always reminds me of the Lord Mayor's Show.

H.G. Newitt

How I was committed to Islam

I was born in a German Christian family during the most ferocious part of World War II, in Berlin, in 1943. My family moved first to Spain, during the same year, and later, in 1948, to Argentina. There I stayed for 15 years. I attended my grade and high school at the Roman Catholic "La Salle" school, in

Cordoba, Argentina. As was to be expected, I became very soon a fervent Catholic. I was lectured over an hour daily on Catholic religion and I often attended religious services. At twelve, my dream was to become a Roman Catholic priest. I was completely committed to the Christian faith.

Allâh observed my folly, and one memorable day, nearly seven years ago, He permitted that a copy of a Spanish translation of the Noble Qur'ân should reach my hands. My father did not object to my reading it, as he supposed that it would only contribute to give me a broader background, and nothing else. He was far from guessing the effect the Words of Allâh were going to exert on my mind ... As I opened the Noble Book, I was a fanatic Roman Catholic; as I closed it, I was completely committed to Islam...

Obviously, my opinion of Islam was not a favorable one before I read the Noble Qur'ân. I took the Holy Book with curiosity, and opened it with scorn, expecting to find in it horrible errors, blasphemies, superstitions and contradictions, I was biased, but I was also very young and my heart had no time to harden completely yet. I went through the *Surâh* reluctantly at the beginning, eagerly then, and finally with a desperate thirst for Truth. Then, in the greatest moment of my life, Allâh gave me His guidance and led me from superstition to Truth, from darkness to Light, from Christianity to Islam... in the blessed pages of the Noble Qur'ân, I found solution to all my problems, satisfaction to all my needs, explication for all my doubts. Allâh attracted me to His Light with irresistible strength, and I gladly yielded

to Him. Everything seemed clear now, everything made sense to me, and I began to understand myself, the universe and Allâh. I was bitterly aware that I had been deceived by my dearest teachers, and that their words were only cruel lies, whether they were aware of it or not. My whole world was shattered in one instant; all concepts had to be revised. But the bitterness in my heart was amply superseded by the ineffable joy of having found my Lord at last, and I was filled with life and gratitude to Him. I still humbly praise and thank Him for His Mercy with me; without His help, I would have remained in darkness and stupidity forever.

Swelled with joy and enthusiasm, I hurried to communicate my findings to other people, to my parents, to my schoolmates, to my instructors... I wanted everybody to know the Truth, to be free of ignorance and prejudice, to feel the joy I felt. I met a fortress surrounding them, a thick wall separating them from the Truth... And I was not able to remove that rampart, because it was in their hearts, harder than stone. I was received with scorn and persecution, unable to understand the blindness of my persecutors. I learned that only Allah can give Light.

The more I learned, the more I felt, compelled to express my gratitude to Allah for having led me to Islam, the Ideal Religion.

I have read sacred Scriptures of every religion; nowhere have I found what I encountered in Islam: perfection. The Holy Qur'ân, compared to any other Scripture I have read, is like

At the Threshold of Islam

the light of the sun compared to that of a match. I firmly believe that anybody who reads the Word of Allah with a mind that is not completely closed to Truth, will become a Muslim, if Allah pleases. He will also travel from darkness to Light...

May Allah grant His Guidance to all the sincere seekers of Truth. The arms of Islam are open to receive them in the heart of a community called by Allah Himself: "the best people that were ever raised for the benefit of mankind."

Praise is to Allah, the Lord of the universe!

Saifuddin Dirk Walter Mosig

U.S.A.

Why I became a Muslim

Deep down in the human soul there lurks the consciousness of the fact that there does exist the All-Mighty God. It is more or less dependent upon the circumstances of education and upbringing under which one is born that our definite religious views are shaped. It was exactly so in my case. My parents were strict Catholics and they brought me up a staunch Catholic, marking me out for the priesthood. But fate would

have it otherwise and my footsteps took me to the country of Java, in the Far East, to observe with my own eyes how dearly and faithfully Muslims held their faith. This was an eyeopener to me; for I learnt that the Muslims, as dinned by the Christian priestcraft, into our ears, are anything but heathens, and Islam which they misrepresented so much is not a religion with hateful practices.

Being a lover of truth, I took up the cudgels for Islam some six years ago, to secure for it its rightful place against untrue and unjust suspicions. I had with this aim in view to call in the help of some distinguished and good-hearted friends for the purpose of building a mosque in Holland in the same way as in London, Berlin, and Paris. Gradually it dawned upon me that it was imperative that the fight for Islam should be maintained. In the meantime, I had learned about Islam from some of my true Muslim friends, and after thoroughly studying the Noble Qur'ân I came to the knowledge that Islam had always been my religion.

The only difference which the present declaration makes is that I am now openly going over to Islam and in this I feel very happy. Now I realize that my place is among my Muslim brothers to glorify Allâh for bringing salvation to mankind.

It does me immense pain to realize why I had not accepted Islam as my faith earlier. I close with the promise that my life from now onwards will be dedicated to the service of the best religion of the world—Islam.

J.L. Ch. Van Beetem, (Mohammad Ali)

At the Threshold of Islam

Why I accepted Islam

I will endeavour in this short article to outline briefly the circumstances which led to my finally embracing Islam, trusting that same may prove of some interest both to my Muslim and non-Muslim readers.

I was brought up from early childhood in an atmosphere of religion, as it was intended that I should ultimately enter the priesthood, but God willed it otherwise, and instead I entered my present profession; therefore, at least, I cannot be accused of taking my consequent step without full knowledge of the facts.

My work and studies having created fresh interests in my life, I naturally found less time at my disposal to devote to religion than hitherto, and, consequently, as time passed finding myself free of the religious influences of my younger days, I began to reason for myself, and eventually I found that I was questioning even the most fundamental principles of a religion which I had until then accepted verbatim; but nevertheless I still continued to fulfill my obligations to God.

About this time came the Great War, and I was drafted with my Regiment on service to the Near East. During this period (some four years) I had the extreme good fortune to make several good friends in Cairo, and it was the result of

discussions I had with these good people, who explained to me certain passages of the Holy Qur'ân, that sowed the seeds in my mind of the doctrines of a religion which I was destined some years later to adopt.

Upon resuming my civil occupation, there followed a period in my life in which, owing to the renewal of my studies and my work, I found little time to devote to the serious study of religious matters; and when I ultimately did, I found that I was no longer able to reconcile myself to the teachings of the Christian Faith, and, as a result, I discontinued my attendance at Church, as I was convinced that any other course under the circumstances was hypocritical.

It was some time later that I recalled to my mind the earlier discussions that I had with my old Egyptian friends, so, in the hope of gaining enlightenment, I devoted a considerable amount of my spare time to a thorough study of an English translation of the Holy Qur'ân, and as I read over and over again certain of the words of the Holy Prophet Muhammad (peace be upon Him!) I could not help but see that here at last in Islam I had found the true faith for which I had been seeking so long. And the knowledge gave me a totally different outlook on life, as if, after groping endlessly about dark and obscure byways, I had at last come upon a bright and illuminated thoroughfare.

It was not long after this that I visited the Mosque at Woking and consulted Maulvi Abdul-Majid, to whom I would like to record my appreciation of his kind advice and assistance, and thereupon joined the Holy Brotherhood of Islam. "All praise

to Allah!" And from that day, needless to say, I have felt a different being, having a purpose in life.

I will not attempt to discuss here the fundamental principles of Islam which I am content to leave in more able hands. There is a point, however, which to my mind deserves mention, as one who has closely followed the religious observances of both Muslims and Christians. That whilst an average Christian having attended Church Service on a Sunday, which is invariably carried through by a Clergyman and in which the worshipper often takes a rather inactive part, he or she considers their obligation to God fulfilled until the following Sunday. Whereas by comparison the Muslim prays regularly each day individually, either in a Mosque or in the privacy of his home, and even when Friday prayers are said in congregation this individuality is still retained, each Muslim praying independently to Allah without the need of any intermediary or elaborate ritual.

I would like to say that I feel confident, that if only people in this and other Western countries can be brought to appreciate the full meaning of Islam, and what it stands for, the ranks of Islam will be daily swelled, only unfortunately there is a vast amount of misapprehension in the minds of many Free Thinkers and others who still cling to their old creed simply because they require the moral courage to abandon a faith, with the principles of which they are at variance, and to embrace Islam.

Not one of the least of these is the idea that Islam is peculiar to

the Oriental races and not adapted for everyday life in Western countries. This is, of course, a wrong notion, but it, nevertheless, exists in the minds of the majority and requires contradiction in a practical form, and that is to publish for the benefit of the uninitiated the fact that members like myself have joined and are still joining the ranks of Islam and thus give added confidence to our potential brethren of tomorrow.

It is, therefore, essential, to my mind, for this reason alone, if no other, that a building, worthy of Islam, should be acquired and maintained in Central London, where all Muslims could meet and, what is more, by publicity non-Muslims should be attracted in numbers to listen to worthy propounds of the Holy Faith and also see the Faithful ones at prayer, thus giving confidence to those who have a wrong conception of Muslim prayers.

Without such an effort as this, numbers will be lost to Islam, as how otherwise are we to get in touch with those who are wavering in their beliefs and are awaiting enlightenment. For surely I am only one example of hundreds of thousands.

What is more, the prestige of Islam is to be borne in mind. The capital of the British Empire and the center of the world without an edifice worthy of Islam? Unbelievable!

Walker H. Williams

At the Threshold of Islam

Islam – my choice

One day, my son with tears in his eyes said: 'I do not want to remain a Christian any longer; I want to be a Muslim; and you, too, my mother, should join this new faith with me.' That was the first time I felt that I had to link myself with Islam. Years passed before I came in contact with the *Imam* of the Berlin Mosque, who introduced me to Islam. I came to recognize that Islam was the true religion for me. Belief in the Trinity of the Christian faith was impossible for me even at my young age of twenty. After studying Islam I also rejected confession, the holiness and recognition of the supreme power of the Pope, baptism, etc., and thus I became a Muslim.

My ancestors were all sincere believers and pious persons. I was brought up in a convent and hence I inherited a religious attitude towards life. This demanded that I should associate myself with one religious system or the other. I was indeed very fortunate and comforted as I decided to join the religion of Islam.

Today I am a very happy grandmother, because I can claim that even my grandchild is a born Muslim.

"Allâh guides whom He pleases to the Right Path."

Mrs. Amina Mosler

Germany

Why I embraced Islam

The family in which I was born and grew up was, from the religious point of view, no different from the generality of British homes. My mother is a Christian but she doesn't practice religious worship and rituals. My father however did not believe in any religion. In my childhood I studied at a religious school and learned the subjects which are taught in English Church schools. Our usual conversation was never even remotely concerned with religion. I don't remember any day of my childhood when I heard the name of God in my home.

While studying at the Church school I was not satisfied with some of the basic beliefs of Christianity especially the concept of Trinity and the belief in Atonement that God or Jesus had ransomed the people and by accepting the cross had atoned for all their sins. I heard many discussions and arguments about these beliefs but whatever I heard seemed to me only one side of the reality while I wanted to know fully. My school was a Christian school but I left it as an unbeliever.

After joining the university I got the chance to be introduced to Muslims. Before that I had neither read nor heard anything about Islam. In fact like other people in the West I also harboured prejudices and misunderstandings about it. But

here in the university, Muslim students explained their basic beliefs to me calmly and in a very nice manner. They answered all my objections and gave me some books to read. In the beginning I just skipped over the pages of these books when I had nothing to do. I only considered them a source of amusement and derision. But when I actually read parts of these books, they slowly reduced my suspicions about Islam.

Then I started reading those books carefully. Their style of presentation and the freshness of explanation and commentary surprised me. I was extremely impressed by the logic and argument with which their concepts of the Creator and the created and life after death were put forward.

After that these Muslim students gave me an English translation of the Noble Qur'ân. However hard I try I cannot fully estimate the impression the Qur'ân left on my heart. Before I finished the third *Surah,* I had prostrated myself before the Creator of the universe. This was my first *Salât (Namâz)* and since that time by the grace of Allah I am a Muslim. I accepted Islam hardly three months after I came to know about it. So I did not know anything more than basic concepts. After that started a lengthy process of questions which I asked my Muslim brothers and argued with them over the details and sections of these questions.

I am often asked about the main reasons which made me accept Islam. It is difficult for me to give a satisfactory answer to this because the example of Islam—as a European Muslim has put it—is like that of a complete and perfect

geometrical pattern whose every part completes its other parts and its real beauty lies in the harmony and cohesion of these parts, and it is this characteristic of Islam which has a profound influence on human beings. Seen from a distance, Islam's deep insight into the generality of things, motives, deeds, its explanations about the Muslim government will amaze you and if you look at its details, you find it an incomparable guide for social life based as it is on straightforward and true ethical values. A Muslim takes the Name of Allah whenever he does anything. And when he remembers Allah, he examines his own self and in this he tries to reach a high standard. In this way the gulf between daily life of the world and the demands of religion is bridged and both sides become proportionate, evenly balanced and essential for each other

.Ayesha Bridget Honey

England

At the Threshold of Islam

An interview with 'Ayesha Kim

'Ayesha Kim is from Korea. She is a steadfast and resolute lady, soft at heart and strong of will. She had been struggling in search of Truth when the golden rays of Islam touched her heart. Ever since she has moved farther and farther on the road to Islam. Today she is known by her Islamic name 'Ayesha. She has become a lighthouse of faith for the ladies of Korea, and in particular for the girl students of that country. She guides them towards the path of Truth. Islam first came to her husband, Imam Mahdevoon, who is now the head of the Union of Muslims in South Korea. Inwardly, however, 'Ayesha was ahead of him in this matter. They both have started together to traverse the path of Truth.

Ayesha was able to discover truth in the thick of the devastating war that was raging when she chose Islam for her religion. She adopted the Islamic name 'Ayesha after the name of the holy wife of the Prophet (may the peace and blessings of Allâh be upon him). She thought that it would be a source of blessing for her. She says:

> "In the face of ever expanding ideological onslaught of the Missionaries in Korea, it was in Islam that I found the truth of assured certainty."

At the Threshold of Islam

'Ayesha was interviewed for one-and-a-half hours in the Korean Islamic Cultural Centre in Jeddah. She was transiting there together with Korean girl students on their way back from Makkah after performing *'Umrah*. When she was asked about her early involvement with Islam, she first kept quiet and closed her eyes, as if she was trying to look for something hidden in the deep recesses of her heart. She then became alert and after heaving a deep breath, said: "The story of my attachment with Islam is prompting me to look back to those early days which I passed in Korea. I belonged to an orthodox family of staunch followers of an ancient Chinese religion. Korea was run down by war. I was then married to Imam Mahdevoon and we both, the husband and wife, were still away from Islam. I had, however, always an inner feeling that we were away from the reality."

The desire for Truth intensifies

"On reaching Korea," continued 'Ayesha, "I became all the more restless in my heart pinning to know the Truth. My inner voice was prompting me that there was one and only one way to reach the Truth; and it was different from all those religions that I had till then come to know about.

"At that time the Korean war burst which compelled us again to be on the move, but this time the journey was within the country. We moved from the South of Korea towards its western seaside up to the port of Pusan. As soon as we came to an end, I told my husband that Faith was the only fortress to save ourselves as well as the society.

"We had a friend called Omar Kim," she said, "he is now dead. He had embraced Islam publicly. He spoke to us when the war was still going on, urging us for the preaching and propagation of Islam and to invite people to accept it. Our mind was influenced by Omar too. Besides, as a result of war, the country was breaking up, not only economically but also morally. False belief and superstitions were at the root of this turmoil. Such were the pitiable conditions then prevailing."

When asked as to what did she think of the worries of her husband before his acceptance of Islam, she smiled and said:

"When my husband consulted me in this regard, I asked him whether it had not dawned on him already that Islam is the only way to guidance? But he was a victim of some unknown fear and apprehension. He was worried as to how shall we two live together thereafter. I told him that when he would accept Islam, Godwilling, he shall find me going with him."

"These words came in very firm tone out of the very depth of my heart. My husband was, therefore, taken by surprise, realising that I was ahead of him in accepting the Truth."

"Our friend Omar and my husband got introduced to several members of the Turkish troops that were then posted in Korea. Every day they would go to meet them some 20 kilometres from Seoul. At long last, the day came when our painful plodding reached its welcome climax. It was on a Friday in the summer of 1955. My husband, in the presence of the Turkish Imam Abdur-Rahman, accepted Islam at the hands of Zuber Kochi and offered Friday prayer. Both these

gentlemen belonged to the Turkish troops."

About children

After this, she directed attention towards her children. She said, "I have only two daughters. I was apprehending difficulty about them, but I realised that after all we, too, had remained away from Islam for long. Nature itself guides. My elder daughter was then 25 years old. She said, 'My heart? It beats in unison with yours, but for the time being I would rather keep quiet until you procure maximum possible information about Islam.' After some time, she too accepted Islam. Her name was changed from Yoong to Jamila. She was married to a Korean Muslim. My younger daughter accepted Islam at the age of 20. She too was married to a Korean Muslim. She lives in Korea near us.

"As for my own family, I have entrusted the whole matter to Allah. May He grant me success in bringing them into the fold of Islam. Despite my meagre means, I have maintained these relations according to Islamic principles.

Calling others

"I have induced many Korean women to accept Islam. I have made them understand how Islam protects the mutual rights of married couples, and how sound is the foundation it provides for family life. All praise be to Allah, I have succeeded in guiding a large number of women to the path of Truth. We arrange get-togethers for ladies newly converted to Islam.

"I myself can speak Arabic with great difficulty, because I began late to learn it. To learn Arabic is a difficult question for newly converted Muslim ladies. To overcome this difficulty, we are trying to establish a Department of Arabic in the Islamic Cultural Centre of Korea."

"Another difficulty is that newly converted Muslim girls have to live in a society in which the majority religion has the upper hand. For this reason, in order to keep up the spirit of these girls, it is essential to organise their effective defence. This defence can come only through Muslim educational institutions."

"For the beginning and as of now, Muslim women in Korea are organised in Seoul only. Welfare meetings are held by them to chalk out programmes for providing assistance to the poor. We have many instances of this. Several newly-wed Muslim couples have dedicated themselves to take the message of Islam to people at large."

Hope for the Future

When asked about her last wish in her advanced age, she said, "All praise be to Allah! My husband, my children and myself, all have accepted Islam. We have performed *Hajj* and *'Umrah* several times. My first pilgrimage tour took place in 1978 when I also took the opportunity to try to understand how life goes on in the Muslim community. Now that I am returning from Saudi Arabia to Korea, I am leaving my heart behind. There is an abiding desire to pay never ending visits to the City of the Holy Prophet, upon him be Allah's blessings

and peace."

At the end of the interview, good wishes were extended to her for all success in her noble mission, and it was concluded on the Qur'ânic Verse:

> "If Allah helps you, none can overcome you..." (*Surah Aal Imran*, 3:160).

'Ayesha Kim

Why I embraced Islam

First and foremost I would say it was because fundamentally I had always been a Muslim without being aware of it.

Very early in my life, I had lost faith in Christianity for many reasons, the major one being that whenever I questioned any Christian, whether it was a person belonging to the so-called Holy Orders or a layman, regarding any point that puzzled me in regard to the Church teachings, I invariably received the monotonous answer: 'You must not question the teachings of the Church; you must have faith.' I did not have the courage in those days to say: 'I cannot have faith in

something that I do not understand,' and, from my experience, neither do most of the people who call themselves Christians. What I did do was to leave the Church (Roman Catholic) and its teaching and to place my faith in the one true God in Whom it was much easier to believe, than in the three gods of the Church. By contrast with the mysteries and miracles of the Christian teaching, life took on a new and wider meaning, no longer cramped with dogma and ritual. Everywhere I looked I could see God's work. And although, in common with greater minds than my own, I could not understand the miracles that happened before my eyes, I could stand and marvel at the wonder of it all—the trees, flowers, birds and animals. Even a newborn baby became a beautiful miracle, not the same thing that the Church had taught me to believe at all. I remembered how, when a child, I gazed at newborn babies and thought, "It's all covered in black sin." I no longer believed in ugliness; everything became beautiful.

Then one day my daughter brought home a book about Islam. We became so interested in it that we followed it up with many other books on Islam. We soon realized that this was really what we believed. During the time I had believed in Christianity, I had been led to believe that Islam was only something to joke about. Thus, all that I then read, was a revelation to me. After a while, I looked up some Muslims and questioned them on some of the points that were not quite clear to me. Here again there was yet another revelation. My questions were all answered promptly and concisely, so different from the frustration I had experienced when

questioning Christianity. After much reading and studying of the religion of Islam both my daughter and myself decided to become Muslims, taking names of Rashida and Mahmuda respectively.

If I were asked what impressed me most in the religion of Islam, I would probably say the prayers, because prayers in Christianity are used wholly in begging God (through Jesus Christ) to grant worldly favors, whereas in Islam they are used to give praise and thanks to All-Mighty Allâh for all His blessings since He knows what is necessary for our welfare and grants us what we need without our asking for it.

Mrs. Cecilia Mahmuda Cannoly

(Australia)

Why Islam is my choice

Islam is the religion I have been seeking since my school-days. My mind was dissatisfied all along with the Christian teachings till I was old enough to have independence of thought to shake them off. Since I left school I have had the opportunity of spending a few years abroad, living with

At the Threshold of Islam

Jewish and Catholic friends, but their religions never appealed to me. Only this year I returned to my native country of Scotland and one day, quite by chance, a friend took me to an "At Home" held at the London Muslim Prayer House, III, Campden Hill Road, Notting Hill Gate, London, W. 8. There it was that I came in touch with the true religion of Islam. I became interested in Islam, whose keynote is implicity—for instance, belief in the Unity of God. This is why, it appeals to me. As a Christian, I could never bring myself to believe in the doctrine of the Trinity, the Atonement,.... Islam is absolutely free from such gross impossibilities that it was necessary for an innocent man like Jesus to come to the world and give his life to save it from sin, as the Christian dogma would have us believe, is beyond my comprehension. Further, the Crucifixion has not made the world any better (except, perhaps, the few who tried to be like him).The world on the other hand, it seems to me, is worse than it was in Jesus Christ's lifetime.

To any thinking person who takes the trouble to understand Islam this simple and noble religion must appeal.

The *Deen* of Islam has given me peace and happiness such as I never had before.

Miss Joan Fatima Dansken

My allegiance to Islam

I was born in a Tatar village in Russia, where my father, a Roman Catholic Pole and an exile from Poland, was a doctor.

Both my parents died early, and I was brought up among the Russian intelligentsia without any religion, principles or traditions. I must say I never gave much thought to spiritual matters until, after having lived in England and America, I imperceptibly became convinced that one must have some guiding principles in one's life and some kind of moral code. I studied Christianity, but, even stripped of all the trappings of ritualism and superstitions, it could not satisfy me because I could not accept the fundamental principles of Christianity—the divinity of Jesus and the doctrine of the original sin and redemption. It seemed to me that the true God was completely overshadowed by the tremendous figure of Christ, and I could not believe that the suffering and death of one person, however saintly, even divine, would redeem the sins of the whole world, especially as the world went on sinning as if nothing happened. So, naturally I turned to Islam. I say naturally because I always had a sort of nostalgia for Islam, brought up, as I was in its atmosphere from my earliest childhood. It was like coming home, and the more I read the Qur'ân and the books on Islam by Muslim writers,—the most lucid and convincing of them being those

of the Khawaja Kamal-ud-Din,—the more I became convinced that it is the only true religion,—a religion for people who think and do not want to shut their eyes to the realities of life and the discoveries of science. I could not help comparing it to the teaching of Jesus which, lofty as it is, either leads to asceticism and virtual denial of life, or demands an enormous structure of casuistry and sophistry in order to adapt it to the earthly life of mankind. How could it stand in comparison with the pure logic of Islam—submission to the will of God and striving towards His perfection? There, one has not the theological dogmas and magic formulas for salvation, but a perfect guidance and a moral code for the whole conduct of life, which does not demand denying the evidence of one's reason, nor the violation of one's natural feelings. Indeed, I cannot understand how any thinking person can fail seeing it. That is why, so many critics of Islam fall back on the "bad life" of the people in Muslim countries, willfully shutting their eyes to the fact that their vices are due not to the teachings of Islam but to the dire poverty and ignorance in which they live owing to the physical and political conditions of their countries. My only regret is that I did not see the truth earlier, as it would not only have made me happier, but would have helped me to become a more useful member of the community.

Mrs. C. Sa'eeda Namier

At the Threshold of Islam

Why I embraced Islam

Shortly after I was born in 1934 it became a "fashion" in Germany to quit membership of the Church—Catholic or Protestant—and become "gottglaubig" which means believing in God but actually signifies rather the contrary. In fact when I was about seven years old, an elder girl told me that there was no God at all and as she seemed to me quite an authentic person and I had just learned that also Santa Claus is only an invention for children, turned all my interest towards this world. Yet the world at that time was far from being easily understandable for young people. There were bombs day after day, there was father who could come only now and then for just one day and mother who knitted gloves and socks for "our poor soldiers," there was a big house in the neighbourhood which was turned into a hospital for the wounded. When that was over, there were strange people who took away our house and American war-films started coming in which melted my heart. I was unable to judge who was right and who was wrong and everything looked cruel and senseless to me—there were a thousand whys to which nobody could give a satisfactory answer. I started to be on the outlook for God yet hard though I tried I could neither find Him in Catholicism nor Protestantism nor with Jehova's Witnesses. The road nearer to God in these religions was barred for me through the fact that all of them had doctrines

in which to believe I found impossible, and injunctions to follow which strictly seemed to me impracticable. And how could I accept a faith in which I knew from the very outset that I would be tortured by self accusation for my own imperfection?

It is still a miracle for me that of all girls, I was the one to meet a young European who had already embraced Islam seven years before. The very first time we met I happened to enquire about his religion and when I learned that it was Islam I asked him to tell me more about it. I was a great sceptic at that time due to the disappointments I had had with other religions, yet when he explained to me the meaning of the word 'Muslim', i.e., one who out of free will surrenders himself to God's Commandments, something started waking up within me. Then he went on to explain to me that all men, animals, plants and everything else in this universe is already Muslim compulsorily because they would destroy themselves if they would not follow God's laws in matters such as eating, drinking, procreation and so on. Man alone, so he said, is in a position to accept Islam also spiritually, apart from the material sphere where he practically does not have a free choice but has to follow his inborn urges as animals and plants.

It was the wonderful logic, the pure commonsense in all Islamic teachings which attracted me so much, in the first few fundamental doctrines about which I learned as much as in the books I read in the following years small though the stock of unbiased Islamic literature in German language is.

Apart from the help of the young Muslim he now is my husband—who never got tired of explaining things to me and answering all my questions. Muhammad Asad's book *"The Road to Mecca"* made me understand the deep meaning behind all Islamic injunctions and thus helped me most while I was on my way to become a *Muslimah*.

Fatima Heeren
West Germany

How I entered Islam

Madame Fatima Mik Davidson is the Minister of State for Social Development and Local Government of the Republic of Trinidad and Tobago. In an interview given by her to the renowned Arabic Magazine *Menbarul-Islam* of Cairo, Madame Fatima Mik Davidson (formerly Mrs. Model Donafamik Davidson) talked about the beginning of her encounter with Islam and how she ultimately turned Muslim. She said:

"I totally deny the idea that I accepted Islam in 1975 by renouncing Christianity. Really I am quite unable to understand and explain what the matter was with me. Let me take you back to the 9th of March, 1950, the day that was fixed for me to enter a Christian Monastery. When I woke up

in the morning of that day, I felt that the voice — الله اكبر الله اكبر (*Allâhu-Akbar Allahu-Akbar*) was ringing in my ears and it was thrilling my entire inner self. Lo! I had come back to Islam.

"I did not quite know what it was, but the monastery I refused to enter. After that I passed many years, seeking Allah's guidance, until at last I was able to come across a copy of the translation of the Holy Qur'ân. Then I readily put faith in it. I happened to meet a Muslim scholar, Maulana Siddiq from Pakistan and an Indian scholar Shaykh Ansari. I had detailed talks with them about nature and what I felt about it in my heart, so much so that these great scholars exclaimed to me: 'Thank Allah you are a Muslim! You are now a Muslim lady. Read what you like, enter the Mosques and pray. We are prepared to welcome you, whenever you feel disposed to learn anything.'"

Iman is Bliss

"I felt happy. Ever since that day I have been feeling that my heart is overflowing with the bliss of *Iman* (Faith) and with love and high esteem for the Holy Prophet Muhammad (may the peace and blessings of Allâh be upon him). Although the date of my formally embracing Islam is sometime in the year 1975, I have been a Muslim for the last 33 years, ever since the day I heard the great mysterious voice and I refused to enter the monastery. My heart proclaimed: الله اكبر (*Allâhu Akbar:* God is the Greatest).

"I was the first coloured girl to enter the Mosque. This

encouraged many Muslim girls to enter Mosques for prayer, particularly the Mosque of the Anjuman Jami' Sanatal which was founded by the great scholar Dr. Shaykh Ansari in the city of Francis in Trinidad. Its present Chairman is Al-Hajj Shafiq Muhammad.

"Prior to this, the residents over there thought that Islam was the religion of the Indians who followed so many shades of religious tenets and paths. They thought Qadianism and Ahmadism being more important.

"Later on a large number of the islanders, mostly of African origin, embraced Islam, until the ratio of the Muslims rose to 13 percent of the total population of the Republic, as against 31 percent Catholics, 27 percent Protestants, 6 percent Hindus, and 23 percent others."

Effect on her Duties

About the effect of her embracing Islam on her work in a state where Muslims are not in the majority, she said:

"Islam demands of us efficient and sincere application to duty and I practise the teachings of the Faith (Islam) with sincerity. I do not tell lies either in my (official) work or in my (personal) life. To the best of my ability and with strong consciousness of my heart I shun everything that is repugnant to Islam. As regard the impact of my conversion upon my work, it was nothing but all blessing and good. Our former Prime Minister advised me to visit Egypt, because it is the land of the renowned Jami'ah Al-Azhar and the source of civilization. He used to talk a great deal about Islam.

At the Threshold of Islam

"When I requested my present Prime Minister to give me permission to visit Egypt in connection with my assignment as Minister of State for Social Development and Local Government, he agreed and also advised me to visit Al-Azhar and the Supreme Council of Islamic Affairs about whose activities we heard so much during our visits to the U.S.A. and the U.K.

"I took part in the parliamentary elections many a time and came out successful in spite of being a Muslim. I have worked as Minister for Education and Culture and also as a Minister in the Prime Minister's Cabinet, although I am a Muslim.

"I would like to tell of something important. The Republic of Trinidad and Tobago allows official holidays on the occasions of *Eid-ul-Fitr* and *Eid-ul-Azha* festivals. The Muslims have freedom to celebrate the month of Ramadan in their houses as well as in the mosques throughout the State."

She further said:

"I make an appeal to the Islamic World to close their ranks because unity is strength, particularly under cover of the excellent religion of Islam which has brought equality to mankind and which regulates our relations and dealings. It is, therefore, imperative that the Islamic World should halt the wars raging among its certain states. It is possible to resolve all difficulties and disputes with mutual negotiations, consultation and understanding.

"Almighty Allah has guided me to Islam and I pray Him to

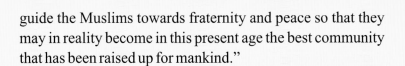

guide the Muslims towards fraternity and peace so that they may in reality become in this present age the best community that has been raised up for mankind."

Madame Fatima Mik Davidson

Minister of State for Social Development
and Local Government,
Republic of Trinidad and Tobago

At the Threshold of Islam